Instant Magento Shipping How-to

Making Magento shipping settings work for your business

Robert Kent

BIRMINGHAM - MUMBAI

Instant Magento Shipping How-to

First published: May 2013

Production Reference: 1170513

Published by Packt Publishing Ltd.
Livery Place
35 Livery Street
Birmingham B3 2PB, UK.

ISBN 978-1-78216-540-8

www.packtpub.com

Credits

Author
Robert Kent

Reviewers
Nayrolles Mathieu

Kalpesh Mehta

Acquisition Editor
Joanne Fitzpatrick

Commissioning Editor
Neha Nagwekar

Technical Editors
Ankita R. Meshram

Zafeer Rais

Project Coordinator
Sneha Modi

Proofreader
Aaron Nash

Production Coordinator
Melwyn D'sa

Cover Work
Melwyn D'sa

Cover Image
Abhinash Sahu

About the Author

Robert Kent is a web developer who specializes in bespoke web development, Magento website creation, Magento extension development, and frontend development work. With 5 years of experience in web development, he has acquired expertise in Magento, Wordpress, PHP, JavaScript, jQuery, HTML, HTML5, CSS3, XML, and the Adobe Creative Suite, as well as knowledge in a whole range of other languages and frameworks. After graduating from university with a first class degree in Multimedia computing, he made the choice to move into web design and development and put the skills he learned to the test.

He currently works at Creare Communications Ltd, a rapidly expanding Web Design and SEO company based in the UK as a Web Development Manager. He is currently focused primarily on R&D for the continued expansion of the company through building systems to help with the management of over 150 employees. He is also a key member of the team working on the company's flagship Magento-powered website `https://www.creare.co.uk`

When not knee-deep in code, he likes a good game of English football, watching a great film with his long-term girlfriend, and fantasizing about fast cars.

About the Reviewers

Mathieu Nayrolles was born in France where he started his studies in Computing Sciences at Cesi.eXia and passed the diploma of Manager of Informations Systems. He traveled across Europe thanks to his various internships, where he learned how to optimize in industrial environments.

For his fourth year of engineering, he decided to follow a double diploma course at UQAM, Québec, Canada. During his study at UQAM, he was awarded for one of his publications *Specification and Detection of SOA Antipatterns* at the *10th International Conference on Service Oriented Computing*. He is still processing his final year in both schools, where he is writing two Masters theses in the fields of Artificial Intelligence and Quality.

He has worked for global companies such as Eurocopter and Saint-Gobain. Currently, Mathieu Nayrolles gives courses on agile development, service oriented architectures, business intelligence, and data mining at bachelor level in UQAM and CESI.eXia, while he pursues his own studies.

Mathieu Nayrolles have also written a book for optimizing Magento stores called Instant *Magento Performance Optimization How-to* published by *Packt Publishing*.

You can find even more about Mathieu Nayrolles at his website, www.mathieu-nayrolles.com.

Kalpesh Mehta is a Magento Certified Developer working for an US company as a Lead Magento Developer. He has over 6 years of experience in open source technologies like PHP/MySQL and 3 years of experience in Magento. He has been helping Magento developers since 2011 through his Magento dedicated blog http://ka.lpe.sh (which is very popular among Magento developers) and frequently answers questions on Stack Overflow. In his free time he likes to take freelance projects and review articles/books written in PHP or Magento framework.

If you would like to reach him, send him an e-mail to k@lpe.sh.

www.PacktPub.com

Support files, eBooks, discount offers and more

You might want to visit www.PacktPub.com for support files and downloads related to your book.

Did you know that Packt offers eBook versions of every book published, with PDF and ePub files available? You can upgrade to the eBook version at www.PacktPub.com and as a print book customer, you are entitled to a discount on the eBook copy. Get in touch with us at service@packtpub.com for more details.

At www.PacktPub.com, you can also read a collection of free technical articles, sign up for a range of free newsletters and receive exclusive discounts and offers on Packt books and eBooks.

http://PacktLib.PacktPub.com

Do you need instant solutions to your IT questions? PacktLib is Packt's online digital book library. Here, you can access, read and search across Packt's entire library of books.

Why Subscribe?

- ▶ Fully searchable across every book published by Packt
- ▶ Copy and paste, print and bookmark content
- ▶ On demand and accessible via web browser

Free Access for Packt account holders

If you have an account with Packt at www.PacktPub.com, you can use this to access PacktLib today and view nine entirely free books. Simply use your login credentials for immediate access.

Table of Contents

Preface

The cost of shipping is one of the most important factors a customer takes into account when placing an order through an e-commerce store. If the shipping cost is surprisingly high, the customer is more likely than not to abandon their cart. As a store owner, you don't want customers abandoning their carts, you want customers to complete their purchase, receive their goods, tell all their friends and relatives about your great service, and come marching straight on back through your virtual doors with pockets bulging with cash.

Magento comes equipped with the tools to be able to offer this level of service by setting up multiple shipping methods and rates, ensuring you are catering for every customer requirement. By communicating through orders, comments, statuses, and customized transactional e-mails, you are breathing personality through your Magento system. Not only this, but also understanding how to configure Magento's shipping settings will make life as a store owner so much easier. No more confusion between an order that's processing but not shipped and an order that's "processing" but not invoiced.

More importantly, we will learn how to set up as many free shipping options as you possibly can—one of the biggest online factors between a customer heading for the exit and a customer sailing straight through the checkout.

What this book covers

Configuring shipping settings (Must know) tells you everything you need to know in terms of setting up a Magento store to work with your chosen shipping method, from configuring tax rules and rates to setting up your shipping origin.

Choosing your shipping method (Must know) explores the differences between the Flat Rate, Table Rates, and Free Shipping methods, as well as teaches you how to disable a shipping method and configure your Table Rates.

Configure your products for shipping (Must know) helps you understand the differences between simple, configurable, grouped, bundle, virtual, and downloadable product types and how they affect your shipping calculations.

Advanced shipping methods (Should know) teaches you how to install a new shipping method, configure and enable it, as well as how to configure the DHL shipping method.

Shipping your orders (Should know) teaches you how to create a new shipment for an order, learn how to append comments to keep in contact with your customer, notify them of any changes, and add a tracking code for your customer to monitor their parcels progress.

Changing order status for shipping stage (Become an expert) explains how to create custom order statuses for your orders in order to remove confusion between shipped orders that all have the same status, but in reality are at different stages of the shipment process.

Shipping promotions and discounts (Become an expert) breaks into the sometimes complicated shopping cart price rules system and helps you create a new free shipping promotion tailored to a certain region using the customers shipping address.

Handling your shipping reports (Become an expert) looks into the built-in Magento shipping reports and how it breaks down the reports into the different orders using different shipping methods.

Customizing your shipping e-mails (Become an expert) explains how the default Magento transactional e-mail templates can be customized easily and assigned to be sent out when a new shipment has been created for an order.

What you need for this book

You'll need a Magento store set up and ready to configure, some of these recipes require Magento 1.5+ (for the *Changing order status for shipping stage* recipe). You'll also need administrator level access or sufficient privileges to edit the paths required in this book.

Who this book is for

Are you in charge of shipping your Magento orders? Are you fed up with losing track of which order has been shipped, which is delayed, and which is complete? Do you want to offer your customers more shipping methods and rates and better promotions? If so then this book provides answers to all of this and more.

This book is aimed at Magento store owners themselves, or those who are in charge of configuring their Magento shipping settings. It is also useful for those who have a good working knowledge of the Magento administration panel, but who wish to further their understanding of how products, orders, and shipments work together.

Conventions

In this book, you will find a number of styles of text that distinguish between different kinds of information. Here are some examples of these styles, and an explanation of their meaning.

Code words in text, database table names, folder names, filenames, file extensions, pathnames, dummy URLs, user input, and Twitter handles are shown as follows: "shipping rates imported via a .csv file are always entered at a website view level"

New terms and **important words** are shown in bold. Words that you see on the screen, in menus or dialog boxes for example, appear in the text like this: "In the **Origin** tab we need to enter the details of our company's warehouse".

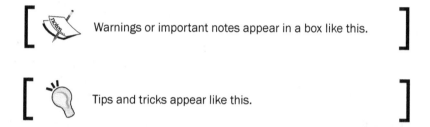

Warnings or important notes appear in a box like this.

Tips and tricks appear like this.

Reader feedback

Feedback from our readers is always welcome. Let us know what you think about this book—what you liked or may have disliked. Reader feedback is important for us to develop titles that you really get the most out of.

To send us general feedback, simply send an e-mail to feedback@packtpub.com, and mention the book title via the subject of your message.

If there is a topic that you have expertise in and you are interested in either writing or contributing to a book, see our author guide on www.packtpub.com/authors.

Customer support

Now that you are the proud owner of a Packt book, we have a number of things to help you to get the most from your purchase.

Errata

Although we have taken every care to ensure the accuracy of our content, mistakes do happen. If you find a mistake in one of our books—maybe a mistake in the text or the code—we would be grateful if you would report this to us. By doing so, you can save other readers from frustration and help us improve subsequent versions of this book. If you find any errata, please report them by visiting http://www.packtpub.com/submit-errata, selecting your book, clicking on the **errata submission form** link, and entering the details of your errata. Once your errata are verified, your submission will be accepted and the errata will be uploaded on our website, or added to any list of existing errata, under the Errata section of that title. Any existing errata can be viewed by selecting your title from http://www.packtpub.com/support.

Piracy

Piracy of copyright material on the Internet is an ongoing problem across all media. At Packt, we take the protection of our copyright and licenses very seriously. If you come across any illegal copies of our works, in any form, on the Internet, please provide us with the location address or website name immediately so that we can pursue a remedy.

Please contact us at copyright@packtpub.com with a link to the suspected pirated material.

We appreciate your help in protecting our authors, and our ability to bring you valuable content.

Questions

You can contact us at questions@packtpub.com if you are having a problem with any aspect of the book, and we will do our best to address it.

Instant Magento Shipping How-to

Welcome to *Instant Magento Shipping How-to*, where you will learn how to tailor Magento's shipping settings to your business; understand how your products and shipping work together, and how to create shipping promotions for your customers.

You will learn how to move on to advanced shipping management for your orders and how to pull your shipping reports straight from Magento.

The recipes contained within this book are based on Magento Version 1.5 to 1.7.0.2, which is the most recent release.

Configuring shipping settings (Must know)

A default Magento installation comes with so many configuration options that it is very easy to miss all of the settings required to effectively set up your shipping options.

Getting ready

To successfully configure our settings, we will need Magento administrator access or at the very least access to **System | Configuration** and also **Sales | Tax**.

We need to ensure that when editing the configuration, our **Current Configuration Scope** field is set to **Default Config**—unless of course we have multiple website views, in which case we should edit the configuration of each website view independently.

It is assumed at this stage that our Magento website is either freshly installed or we are missing our basic configuration options.

The next steps might seem daunting at first, but they are simple to follow and performed in the most logical order. As we work our way through the steps, we should start to understand the scale of configuration options that we can perform on a Magento website in terms of setting up our shipping.

How to do it...

1. To first make sure that our store information is correct, navigate to **System | Configuration** and click on the **General** tab.

2. Within the **Store Information** tab, we need to enter our default store information such as **Store Name**, **Store Contact Telephone**, **Country**, **VAT Number** (if applicable), and **Store Contact Address**. The following screenshot shows example data that you can use for this section:

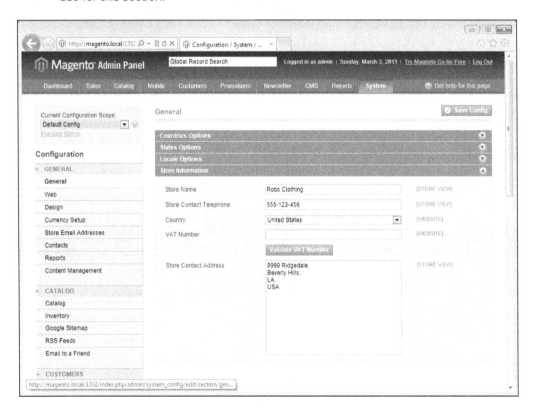

3. Next we need to configure our shipping settings, so let's first navigate to **System | Configuration** and click on the **Shipping Settings** tab. If the **Shipping Settings** tab is not visible, we need to check that our **Current Configuration Scope** field is not set to a store view.

4. In the **Origin** tab we need to enter the details of our company's warehouse (the location where we will be dispatching our customers' orders).

 It is important to enter the origin information as it may be used in our shipping tax calculations, also if we fail to enter our shipping origin, our Magento installation may not calculate product tax correctly within the administration area.

5. Within the **Options** section set **Allow Shipping to Multiple Addresses** to Yes or No (depending on whether you want to give your customers the ability to split their order items and have them shipped to different locations).

6. Next we need to set up our shipping tax rates, so let's navigate to **System | Configuration** and click on the **Tax** tab.

7. Within **Tax Classes** let's select **Shipping** as our tax class (Magento provides this class for us by default).

8. Inside the **Calculation Settings** tab we now need to set **Tax Calculation Based On** to **Shipping Address** (if we set this to **Shipping Origin** then all shipping tax would be calculated from our origin address). Finally, we'll set **Shipping Prices** to **Including Tax**. We can leave all other settings as default within the **Calculation Settings** tab.

9. Next, perform the following steps on both the **Shopping Cart Display Settings** and **Orders, Invoices, Credit Memos Display Settings** tabs.

10. Firstly, set the **Display Shipping Amount** field to **Including and Excluding Tax** and then set the **Display Full Tax Summary** option to **Yes**. The following screenshot shows the **Calculation Settings** and **Shopping Cart Display Settings** tabs completed:

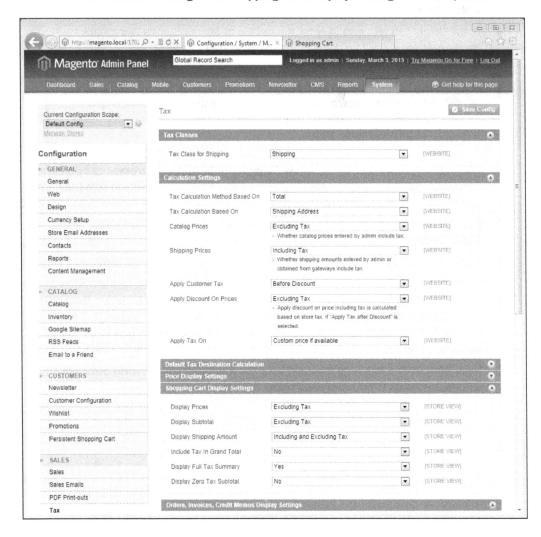

11. After ensuring that our tax settings are correct, we now need to create our tax class and shipping tax rates, so let's navigate to **Sales | Tax | Manage Tax Zones & Rates** and click on **Add New Tax Rate**.

12. Within this section let's set **Tax Identifier** to **US Shipping Tax**, **Country** to **United States**, **State** to ***** (this means any state), **Zip/Post is Range** to **No**, enter * in **Zip/Post Code** (this means any zip/postal code), and finally lets set **Rate Percent** to **10.0000**. The following screenshot shows our complete tax rate information:

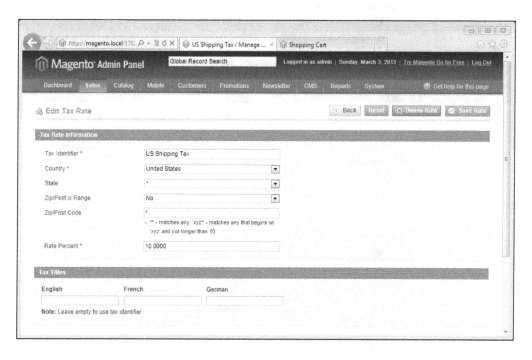

13. We can leave the **Tax Titles** entries blank, as this will force our **Tax Identifier** field to be the title for our new rate. Click on **Save Rate** to save the rate and then we can move on to applying it to a new tax rule.

14. To apply our new rate to a tax rule, navigate to **Sales | Tax | Manage Tax Rules** and then click on **Add New Tax Rule**.

15. Let's now enter the information for our new rule. For **Name** enter US Shipping Rule, for **Customer Tax Class** select **Retail Customer**, for **Product Tax Class** select **Shipping**, and for **Tax Rate** select **US Shipping Tax**. The rest of the fields can be left as default. To save our new rule click on **Save Rule**. The following screenshot shows our tax rule information all filled out:

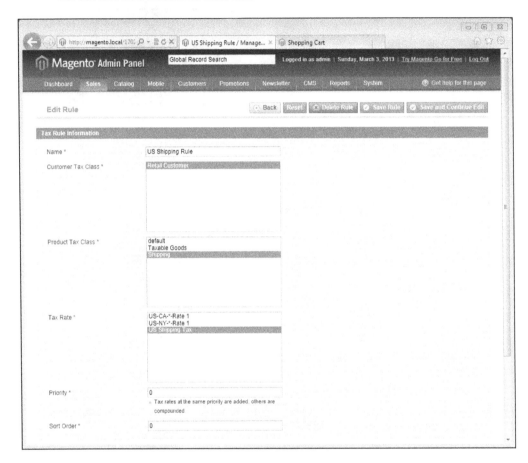

How it works...

Inside our **Store Information** tab we enter our default store information. These details are important as Magento uses this information to automatically populate some sections of its e-mail templates.

The **Shipping Origin** field is sometimes used by Magento's tax calculation settings depending on whether we use our shipping origin or the customers' address details to calculate our tax information. For this reason it is important that we enter this information accurately as the country and region settings will match up with our tax rules and rates.

The **Multi-Shipping** setting enables Magento to use a multi-shipping checkout experience that is different to the standard One-Page checkout we are familiar with. If we were to enable multi-shipping then our customers would be able to choose which items get shipped to which address.

From an administration point of view, a customer that purchases items on the website using the multi-shipping checkout option will produce a separate order for each of the addresses that they chose to deliver an item to.

When processing the orders, we need to be conscious of the fact that multi-shipping orders may have come from the same customer but are saved with separate order numbers and different shipping addresses.

By configuring our shipping tax settings we are dramatically affecting the way Magento calculates the shipping cost and tax implications for a customer's order. For instance, the **Tax Calculation Based On** setting will use the location of either the customer's shipping address (most logical as it's where we are shipping to), billing address, or alternatively our origin—calculating the tax rates based upon the countries and states provided in each of those locations.

The **Shipping Prices** setting determines whether the price of the shipping that we input (within any of our shipping methods) include or exclude tax.

Within our **Display Settings** tab we configure what the customer sees when they are on the shopping cart page—checkout or viewing their order details. By changing these settings we can affect the customer-facing breakdown of our shipping charges in each of those locations.

Shipping tax rates and rules are the most important pieces of the puzzle with regard to enabling tax on your shipping charges. It can be quite complicated at first to understand how the configurations of our tax settings link in with the created rates and rules.

Essentially, what we are doing is applying a percentage charge based on country and state (our tax rate) to a new rule. This rule applies the charge only if certain criteria are met—in our example that would be a retail customer purchasing from our store. The rate is then applied to our **Product Tax Class** field where we selected **Shipping** that we have chosen as the overriding rule to handle shipping tax when we set our shipping tax settings.

There's more...

We have now successfully set up our shipping settings and tax information; however we have only just scratched the surface of what Magento provides for us when customizing our Magento store for shipping.

What we have learned is that country and state can affect the tax rate that is applied to shipping, therefore it is also true that we can create as many tax rates as we like for any other country and apply them under a rule—meaning that customers from different countries can be charged different tax rates (as long as our tax settings indicate that rates should be applied based on shipping address).

Setting up tax rules for different customer groups

In our example we selected **Retail Customer** from our **Customer Tax Class** section; however we could also apply a new shipping tax rule for a wholesale customer.

To do this we first need to create a new **Customer Tax Class** section by performing the following steps:

1. Navigate to **Sales | Tax | Customer Tax Classes** and click on **Add New**.
2. Within **Class Name** enter Wholesale and then click on **Save Class**.

Now in our tax rules we can select the wholesale customer; in this case we would probably create a new tax rate of a lesser percentage of perhaps 6 percent. We would then select our **Wholesale Customer Tax Class**, our **Shipping Product Tax Class**, and our new rate to provide shipping tax discounts for our wholesale customers.

Different origins for different websites

As Magento allows you to have different websites all running from the same installation, it is possible to change your shipping origin per website.

For example we currently have our US website with the **Shipping Origin** country set to **United States**. If we have a French website, we could change our **Current Configuration Scope** field to our French website and change our **Shipping Origin** country to **France**.

This is important if for example, your business has a warehouse in the USA and a warehouse in France and we have set the **Tax Calculation Based On** field to **Shipping Origin** in our tax settings.

If this were the case, our USA store would use one set of tax rates for all transactions and our French store could use a different set of rates—even if we only have the one tax rule for our shipping.

As long as both rates were selected, Magento would automatically apply the correct rate because it will match the **Shipping Origin** field to the country set within that rate.

Choosing your shipping method (Must know)

Magento comes equipped with a variety of shipping methods—most of which can be used for almost any type of online store.

Getting ready

To view and edit our shipping methods we must first navigate to **System | Configuration | Shipping Methods**. Remember, our **Current Configuration Scope** field is important as shipping methods can be set on a per website scope basis.

There are many shipping methods available by default, but the main generic methods are **Flat Rate**, **Table Rates**, and **Free Shipping**.

By default, Magento comes with the Flat Rate method enabled. We are going to start off by disabling this shipping method.

Be careful when disabling shipping methods; if we leave our Magento installation without any active shipping methods then no orders can be placed—the customer would be presented with this error in the checkout:

Sorry, no quotes are available for this order at this time.

Likewise through the administration panel manual orders will also receive the error.

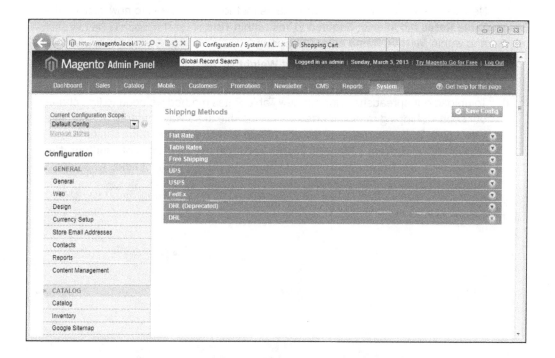

How to do it...

1. To disable our Flat Rate method we need to navigate to its configuration options in **System | Configuration | Shipping Methods | Flat Rate** and choose **Enabled** as **No**, and click on **Save**. The following screenshot highlights our current configuration scope and disabled Flat Rate method:

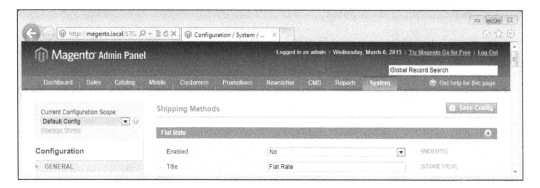

2. Next we need to configure our Table Rates method, so we need to now click on the **Table Rates** tab and set **Enabled** to **Yes**, within **Title** enter `National Delivery` and within **Method Name** enter `Shipping`.

3. Finally, for the **Condition** option select **Weight vs. Destination** (all the other information can be left as default as it will not affect our pricing for this scenario).

4. To upload our spreadsheet for our new Table Rates method we need to first change our scope (shipping rates imported via a `.csv` file are always entered at a website view level). To do this we need to select **Main Website** (this wording can differ depending on **System | Manage Stores Settings**) from our **Current Configuration Scope** field. The following screenshot shows the change in input fields when our configuration scope has changed:

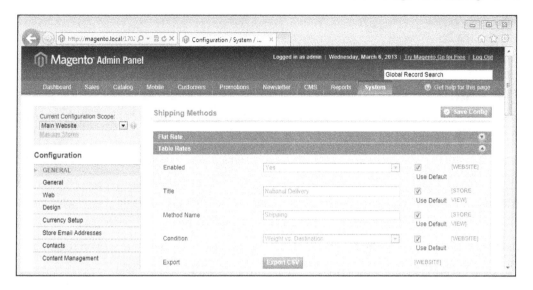

5. Click on the **Export CSV** button and we should start downloading a blank `.csv` file (or if there are rates already, it will give us our active rates).

6. Next we will populate our spreadsheet with the following information (shown in the screenshot) so that we can ship to anywhere in the USA:

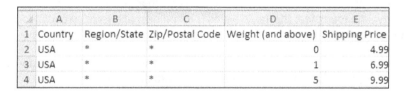

	A	B	C	D	E
1	Country	Region/State	Zip/Postal Code	Weight (and above)	Shipping Price
2	USA	*	*	0	4.99
3	USA	*	*	1	6.99
4	USA	*	*	5	9.99

7. After finishing our spreadsheet we can now import it, so (with our **Current Configuration Scope** field set to our **Website** view) click on the **Choose File/Browse** button and upload it. Once the browser has uploaded the file we can click on **Save**.

8. Next we are going to configure our Free Shipping method to run alongside our Table Rates method, so to start with we need to switch back to our **Default Config** scope and then click on the **Free Shipping** tab

9. Within this tab we will set **Enabled** to **Yes** and **Minimum Order Amount** to **50**. We can leave the other options as default.

How it works...

The following is a brief explanation of each of our main shipping methods.

Flat Rate

The Flat Rate method allows us to specify a fixed shipping charge to be applied either per item or per order.

The Flat Rate method also allows us to specify a handling fee—a percentage or fixed amount surcharge of the flat rate fee.

With this method we can also specify which countries we wish to make this shipping method applicable for (dependent solely on the customers' shipping address details).

Unlike the Table Rates method, you cannot specify multiple flat rates for any given region of a country nor can you specify flat rates individually per country.

Table Rates

The Table Rates method uses a spreadsheet of data to increase the flexibility of our shipping charges by allowing us to apply different prices to our orders depending on the criteria we specify in the spreadsheet.

Along with the liberty to specify which countries this method is applicable for and giving us the option to apply a handling fee, the Table Rates method also allows us to choose from a variety of shopping cart conditions.

The choice that we select from these conditions affects the data that we can import via the spreadsheet. Inside this spreadsheet we can specify hundreds of rows of countries along with their specific states or Zip/Postal Codes. Each row has a condition such as weight (and above) and also a specific price.

If a shopping cart matches the criteria entered on any of the rows, the shipping price will be taken from that row and set to the cart.

In our example we have used Weight vs. Destination; there are two other alternative conditions which come with a default Magento installation that could be used to calculate the shipping:

- ▶ **Price vs. Destination**: This Table Rates condition takes into account the **Order Subtotal (and above)** amount in whichever currency is currently set for the store
- ▶ **# of Items vs. Destination**: This Table Rates condition calculates the shipping cost based on the **# of Items (and above)** within the customer's basket

Free Shipping

The Free Shipping method is one of the simplest and most commonly used of all the methods that come with a default Magento installation.

One of the best ways to increase the conversion rate through your Magento store is to offer your customers Free Shipping. Magento allows you to do this by using its Free Shipping method.

Selecting the countries that this method is applicable for and inputting a minimum order amount as the criteria will enable this method in the checkout for any matching shopping cart. Unfortunately, you cannot specify regions of a country within this method (although you can still offer a free shipping solution through table rates and promotional rules).

Our configuration

As mentioned previously, the Table Rates method provides us with three types of conditions. In our example we created a table rate spreadsheet that relies on the weight information of our products to work out the shipping price.

Magento's default Free Shipping method is one of the most popular and useful shipping methods and its most important configuration option is **Minimum Order Amount**. Setting this value to 50 will tell Magento that any shopping cart with a subtotal greater than $50 should provide the Free Shipping method for the customer to use; we can see this demonstrated in the following screenshot:

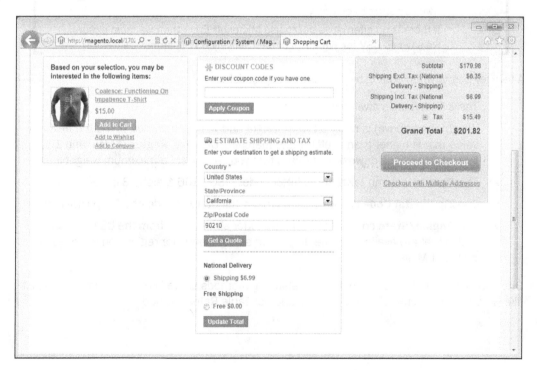

The enabled option is a standard feature among nearly all shipping method extensions. Whenever we wish to enable or disable a shipping method, all we need to do is set it to **Yes** for enabled and **No** to disable it.

Once we have configured our Table Rates extension, Magento will use the values inputted by our customer and try to match them against our imported data. In our case if a customer has ordered a product weighing 2.5 kg and they live anywhere in the USA, they will be presented with our $6.99 price. However, a drawback of our example is if they live outside of the USA, our shipping method will not be available.

The `.csv` file for our `Weight vs. Destination` spreadsheet is slightly different to the spreadsheet used for the other Table Rates conditions. It is therefore important to make sure that if we change our condition, we export a fresh spreadsheet with the correct column information.

One very important point to note when editing our shipping spreadsheets is the format of the file—programs such as Microsoft Excel sometimes save in an incompatible format.

It is recommended to use the free, downloadable Open Office suite to edit any of Magento's spreadsheets as they save the file in a compatible format.

We can download Open Office here:

`www.openoffice.org`

If there is no alternative but to use Microsoft Excel then we must ensure we save as **CSV for Windows** or alternatively **CSV (Comma Delimited)**.

A few key points when editing the Table Rates spreadsheet:

- The * (Asterisk) is a wildcard—similar to saying ANY
- Weight (and above) is really a FROM weight and will set the price UNTIL the next row value that is higher than itself (for the matching **Country**, **Region/State**, and **Zip/Postal Code**)—the downside of this is that you cannot set a maximum weight limit
- The **Country** column takes three-letter codes—ISO 3166-1 alpha-3 codes
- The **Zip/Postal Code** column takes either a full USA ZIP code or a full postal code
- The **Region/State** column takes all two-letter state codes from the USA or any other codes that are available in the drop-down select menus for regions on the checkout pages of Magento

One final note is that we can run as many shipping methods as we like at the same time—just like we did with our Free Shipping method and our Table Rates method.

For more information on setting up the many shipping methods that are available within Magento please see the following link:

```
http://innoexts.com/magento-shipping-methods
```

We can also enable and disable shipping methods on a per website view basis, so for example we could disable a shipping method for our French store.

Disabling Free Shipping for French website

If we wanted to disable our Free Shipping method for just our French store, we could change our **Current Configuration Scope** field to our French website view and then perform the following steps:

1. Navigate to **System | Configuration | Shipping Methods** and click on the **Free Shipping** tab.

2. Uncheck **Use Default** next to the **Enabled** option and set **Enabled** to **No**, and then click on **Save Config**.

We can see that Magento normally defaults all of our settings to the **Default Config** scope; by unchecking the **Use Default** checkbox we can edit our method for our chosen store view.

Configuring your products for shipping (Must know)

There are (by default) six different product types within Magento. Each product type is evaluated and treated differently when Magento comes to work out its shipping charges, so it is important to understand the differences between these product types and how they affect the way Magento processes its shipping charges.

Getting ready

We should be somewhat familiar with the simple/configurable product creation page, where to edit the attributes, and a sense of what attributes are to be expected on these pages. In the following example we will create a virtual product to demonstrate the different product creation page that virtual/downloadable product types display compared to that of another product type.

How to do it...

1. Navigate to **Catalog | Manage Products** and click on **Add Product**.

2. Within **Create Product Settings**, for the **Attribute Set** field select **Default**, set the **Product Type** field to **Virtual Product**, and then click on **Continue**.

3. Notice the lack of a **Weight** attribute and rather simplified **General Settings** tab in the following screenshot:

How it works...

If we create this virtual product and then add it to the cart, we would see that Magento has chosen not to display any shipping information; we've even had our shipping calculator removed from the cart page and there is no longer any option for multi-address shipping.

Likewise, if we were to create a downloadable product, we would get a similar outcome. Further to this, the downloadable and virtual product types remove the shipping address step from our checkout, making it easier for customers to checkout.

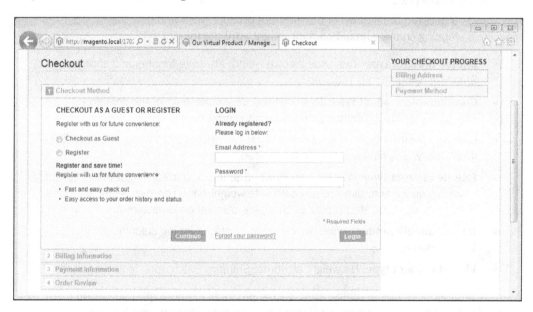

The other product types such as simple/configurable/bundle and grouped products all feature a weight attribute for use in Magento's shipping charge calculation.

Attributes affecting shipping charges

We've already seen that the weight attribute is used within the Table Rates method for Magento to calculate the shipping charges. The other attribute that by default affects the shipping charges within Magento is the price attribute.

Normally, all shipping methods take into account the combined subtotal (calculation of all prices of all products in the cart) as the basis for working out price-based shipping charges. The **Free Delivery Minimum Order Amount** option uses this calculation, as does the **Table Rates Price vs. Destination** condition.

The number of items can also affect the shipping charges if this condition is selected for our Table Rates method. However this is not referring to the inventory of our product but the quantity of products added to the shopping cart.

There's more...

Not only does the choice of product type affect the customer's checkout operation, but it also impacts on our manual order creation process in the Magento administration panel.

Differences between product types, weight attribute, and shipping charges

Following is a detailed breakdown of the different product types and how they affect Magento's shipping charges based on their weight attribute (or lack of):

- ▶ **Simple product type**: This uses its own weight attribute for shipping charges. Shipping calculation is required.
- ▶ **Configurable product type**: This uses the weight attribute of the configured associated product. Shipping calculation is required.
- ▶ **Grouped product type**: This uses the weight attributes of all associated products individually. Shipping calculation is required.
- ▶ **Bundle product type**: We can specify whether to use a fixed weight in the parent bundle product or to dynamically calculate weight based on the weight attribute of all chosen associated products. Shipping calculation is required.
- ▶ **Downloadable product type**: No weight attribute. Shipping calculation is not required.
- ▶ **Virtual product type**: No weight attribute. Shipping calculation is not required.

A virtual product does not, in reality, exist. Virtual products are normally used as an extra charge for items such as warranties or installation charges where no product will be shipped but stock information and reports based on these virtual products should be maintained.

The lack of a weight attribute is important as discussed previously in the *Choosing your shipping method (Must know)* recipe when we were talking about the Table Rate method. With the weight-based table rate enabled, Magento will try to calculate the entire weight of the shopping cart and deliver a price to the customer; normally the miscalculation of the weight will return an error for the shipping charge and the customer will not be able to proceed with the order. Virtual and downloadable products can bypass this required shipping step, but only if they are ordered alone, the combination of a virtual/downloadable product and another product type will result in the shipping information being required once more.

When creating a new order (within **Sales | Orders** and clicking on **Create New Order**) consisting of both downloadable/virtual products and no other types, we will see that the shipping options are also blocked from our input.

Advanced shipping methods (Should know)

When managing a Magento store, it is good to know that we can extend our default installation to bring in new shipping methods by installing extensions. This brings new functionality and a wide range of shipping options to our installation to better serve our customers. These extensions can either enhance the calculations that we provide to our customers such as the Matrix Rates extension, or integrate into third-part carriers such as DHL.

Getting ready

First of all we will install the (free) WebShopApps Matrix Rate extension. The easiest way to do this is to visit their website:

```
http://www.webshopapps.com/us/free/matrixrate-shipping-extension.html
```

Once we have purchased the extension we can download it from our account area and upload it to our Magento website via FTP (if you do not have FTP access please ask your developer to do this for you).

 Once installed we must make sure we clear our cache and (for good measure) log out and then log in again from the administration panel to avoid any permission problems.

We should now find our new **Webshopapps Matrix Rates** extension within **System |
Configuration | Shipping Methods**—handily above our Table Rates method:

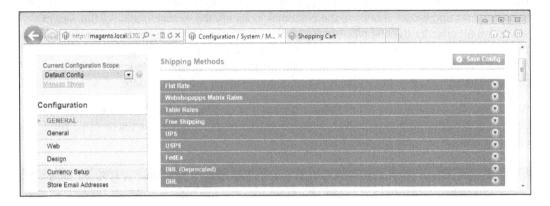

DHL comes pre-installed in Magento, so we do not need to install this separately; however we
do require a DHL account so that we can enter the required information into our configuration.

How to do it...

1. Navigate to **System | Configuration | Shipping Methods** within the **Current
    Configuration Scope** field set to **Default Config** and then click on the **Shipping
    Methods** tab.

2. Click on the **Webshopapps Matrix Rates** section and set **Enabled** to **Yes, Condition**
    to **Weight vs. Destination, Free Shipping Promotions** to **Enable**, and **Only Display
    Free Shipping** to **No**.

3. Within our **Free Shipping Display Text,** enter `Free (within 10 working days)`
    and then set the **Minimum Order Amount For Free Shipping** field to 100, we can
    leave all the other options as default and then click on **Save Config**.

4. Now we need to change our **Current Configuration Scope** field to **Main Website** and
    then click on **Export** to download the `.csv` file (just as we would for Table Rates).
    Once we've edited and uploaded our spreadsheet, our Matrix Rates will be ready
    to use.

5. Next we need to configure our DHL method by firstly changing our **Current
    Configuration Scope** field back to **Default Config** and by clicking on the **DHL**
    tab (not **DHL Deprecated**).

6. Within the **DHL** tab let's set **Enabled for Checkout** to **Yes** and enter our DHL access ID, password, and account number.

7. For our **Content Type** field let's select **Non documents** (unless we are delivering documents) and then set the **Weight Unit** to **Kilograms**.

8. Within **Allowed Methods** we should only choose those that we wish to provide to our customers. The other options we can specify manually if we wish to narrow down the delivery options.

 For a more detailed explanation of all the configuration options please visit http://www.magentocommerce.com/knowledge-base/entry/ shipping-carriers-dhl

How it works...

A few reasons to use the WebShopApps Matrix Rates extension are outlined as follows:

▸ Allows us to specify multiple shipping methods for each rate configuration

▸ Allows us to specify between ranges (ZIP/post codes as well as weights and prices, and so on)

▸ Comes equipped with its own Free Shipping method

There are positives and negatives for using the Matrix Rate extension, but for most purposes the configuration options it provides for free are far superior to those found within the Table Rates method.

The highlight of the Matrix Rates extension has got to be the multiple methods we can use for any given shipping scenario.

For example if we were to ship to anywhere in the USA for weights between 0 and 20 kg, we might want to provide a couple of delivery choices at different costs to the customer as shown in the following screenshot:

	A	B	C	D	E	F	G	H	I
1	Country	Region/State	City	Zip/Postal Code From	Zip/Postal Code To	Weight From	Weight To	Shipping Price	Delivery Type
2	USA	*	*	*	*	0	20	9.99	USA 3-5 Day
3	USA	*	*	*	*	0	20	14.99	USA Next-Day

This spreadsheet will then present the user with two shipping choices—resolving from the one shipping method. As we have configured a free shipping method as well for orders above $100 we should see the following screenshot:

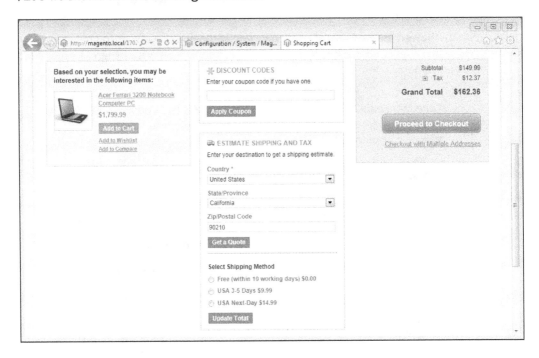

DHL is one of the largest and most widely used shipping methods across the world and therefore it is of no surprise that Magento has decided to grant users the option to connect with DHL within its administration panel.

Unlike the other default shipping methods within Magento, the DHL method will automatically calculate the shipping cost based on the customer's shopping cart and our configuration of each product weight attribute. Therefore we do not need to input any complicated Weight vs. Destination data.

There's more...

Not only does the Matrix Rates extension come equipped with its own Free Shipping method and replicate conditions for Table Rates, it also gives us more control over the names of the shipping methods that we display to the user.

The DHL method is also extremely useful if our store is selling one type of product, this is because it also gives us the option to specify the correct dimensions of our packages. Unfortunately, by default we cannot provide this data per product—only per order.

Free shipping to specific UK postcode

As the Matrix Rates extension is a free extension there are limitations—such as the inability to properly map the from/to postal code ranges. However it does give us more flexibility with regard to whether we want to allow free shipping for a specific UK postcode. For example, we uploaded a spreadsheet that looks as follows:

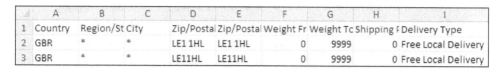

	A	B	C	D	E	F	G	H	I
1	Country	Region/St	City	Zip/Postal	Zip/Postal	Weight Fr	Weight Tc	Shipping F	Delivery Type
2	GBR	*	*	LE1 1HL	LE1 1HL	0	9999	0	Free Local Delivery
3	GBR	*	*	LE11HL	LE11HL	0	9999	0	Free Local Delivery

We would be able to offer the Free Local Delivery method for anyone with that specific postcode. Notice the use of a space and a non-space version of the ZIP/postal code—unfortunately, the extension does not do a good job in anticipating a customer's choice of input.

In some versions of the Matrix Rates extension however, it is possible to use a percentage sign (%) to map for the rest of a postcode, for example, `LE1%`. However we can guess that this might cause a problem in our example as LE11 would also be mapped in that statement.

If we require the ability to map complicated ZIP/postal code ranges or the ability to use formulae within our spreadsheets, we may wish to upgrade to the premium version of this extension.

Shipping your orders (Should know)

Being the owner of a Magento store and receiving orders is one thing, but converting our Magento store into a successful business relies on being able to manage the orders we receive effectively and being able to distinguish between the different stages of an order's lifespan within Magento.

Getting ready

Every order that comes into Magento will appear within our **Sales | Orders** section inside the administration panel.

Within this section we will be shown a complete list of all orders, the associated customer, price, and most importantly their status.

When we are editing an order, we simply select the order by clicking on it. This will take us to the view order page.

So, we have received an order through Magento, the customer's money has been collected by our payment gateway, we have invoiced the customer, and we have done all the hard work behind the scenes picking, packaging, and having our order collected by our chosen carrier. Now we need to mark our order as complete in order to distinguish it from all our other unshipped orders.

How to do it...

1. To ship our order, when on our order view page, we can simply click on the button marked as **Ship**. This will take us to the **New Shipment** page where we will save our shipment for this order.

2. To add a tracking number to our order we need to navigate to the **Shipping Information** section of our new shipment.

3. Within this section we'll set **Carrier** to **DHL**, and within the **Title** field enter DHL.

4. For the **Number** option we need to enter our tracking number obtained from DHL. Once entered we can then click on **Add Tracking Number**. The following screenshot shows the shipping information area:

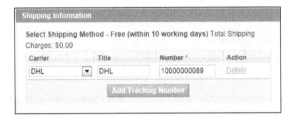

5. Now that we have added our tracking number we can then choose to add a comment to our shipment. Let's navigate down to the comments box and add one as shown in the following screenshot:

6. Once we are happy with our comments we can submit our shipment, navigate to the bottom-right of the page within the yellow box, and then check **Append Comments**, **Email Copy of Shipment**, and finally click on **Submit Shipment** to save our new shipment.

How it works...

Magento's order system heavily relies on order statuses. Whenever we change an order, whether that is invoicing or shipping, the order status should change. By default, once we have invoiced and shipped our order, the order status will change from **Pending** to **Processing** (depending on payment method used).

When we create a new shipment, we are changing the status of our order as well as automatically e-mailing the customer with their tracking code (plus any comments that we decided to add).

It is important to conform to the order processes that Magento provides for us as it makes running our business so much easier, such as generating financial reports and keeping customers up to date throughout the order process.

Now that a new shipment has been created for our order we can always refer back to it by navigating to **Sales | Shipments** (for a complete list of all our shipments) or alternatively, by navigating back through our order to the **Shipments** tab and clicking on the shipment we find there.

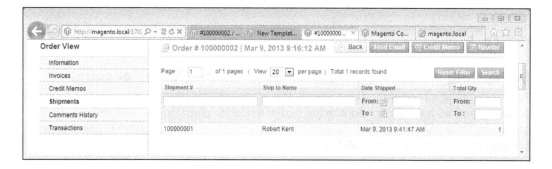

Upon returning to the shipment page for our order we will be able to add more comments or send additional tracking information to the customer as required.

If we are using a carrier such as DHL, they should provide us with a tracking number once they have received our order notification. If we are not using a courier that provides a tracking code or one that isn't supported in Magento, we can choose to not supply one at all.

There's more...

In the **Shipping Information** section there are a number of pre-configured carriers available, each one provides a different link for the customer to click on to track their parcel. Some third-party extensions for other carriers also populate this area with a link for their own tracking number.

Once we have entered our tracking number and saved our shipment, we will be able to track our order by clicking on the **Track this shipment** link on our shipment page as shown in the following screenshot:

Shipment comments can be viewed by the customer within their account section as long the **Visible on Frontend** checkbox is ticked before submitting a comment.

Submitting a shipment comment and viewing in my account

For this example we will enter a comment in the administration panel communicating to the customer that we have confirmed with the carrier that their parcel will be with them in the afternoon. On our view shipment page let's submit a comment similar to that in the following screenshot (making sure that **Visible on Frontend** is checked):

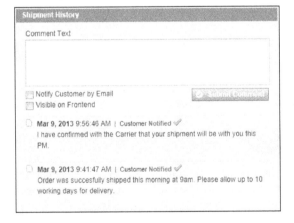

If we could then log in as that customer, we would notice that inside their **My Account** section and within **My Orders** is a tab for shipments that contains our new comment as shown in the following screenshot:

About Your Shipment

Mar 9, 2013 9:56:46 AM

I have confirmed with the Carrier that your shipment will be with you this PM.

Submitting an order comment

Similarly, we can submit a comment for our whole order by visiting the view order page (**Sales | Orders** and clicking on our order) and entering our comment there—the customer will then pick this up in their **My Orders** section of **My Account**.

This would be useful if for example, we wanted to let the customer know that their entire order has been delayed for some reason.

Changing order status for shipping stage (Become an expert)

By default, Magento provides us with some generic order statuses that we can use to distinguish each of the real-life stages our orders are in. As of Magento 1.5 onwards, we have the ability to create our own order statuses.

Getting ready

First of all we are going to take a look at the default order statuses within Magento. To do this we will navigate to **System | Order Statuses**. Within this section we will see a list similar to the following screenshot:

Status	Status Code
Processing	processing
Pending Payment	pending_payment
Payment Review	payment_review
Suspected Fraud	fraud
Pending	pending
On Hold	holded
Complete	complete
Closed	closed
Canceled	canceled
Pending PayPal	pending_paypal

Some of these such as **Processing, Pending Payment, On Hold, Complete**, and **Cancelled** will be familiar to us.

Depending on our Magento setup and which payment gateway we are using, our orders may start off as either **Pending** or **Processing** (payment gateways that take credit card details and transfer the funds instantly via an IPN normally set orders to **Processing**).

In the previous chapter we learned that we could add a comment to an order to let the customer know that their shipment has been delayed. However from an administrative point of view, an order comment does not help us distinguish our delayed orders from our healthy orders when we are looking at a list of them within **Sales | Orders**. Only by clicking on each order and reading the comments can we find out which are delayed.

By creating a new order status called **delayed** we could immediately identify the problematic orders within our list.

How to do it...

1. To create a new order status called delayed we must first navigate to **System | Order Statuses** and click on **Create New Status**.

2. Within **Status Code** enter delayed, in **Status Label** enter Delayed then click on **Save Status.**

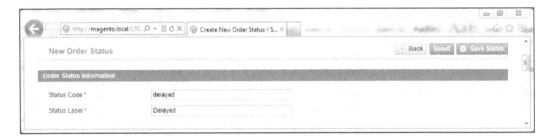

3. Next we need to assign our new status to a state, so let's navigate back to **System | Order Statuses** and click on **Assign Status to State**.

4. For **Order Status** select **Delayed** and then for **Order State** select **Processing**. We can leave **Use Order Status as Default** unchecked and then click on **Save Status Assignment**:

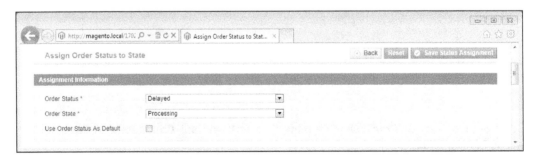

5. To use our new status we must navigate into a new order that has its status currently set to **Processing**. Within the order, navigate to the **Comments History** box and change the **Status** drop-down to our new custom status **Delayed**.

6. All that's left to do is to select whether we wish to **Notify the Customer by Email** (choosing this will send an e-mail to the customer with the current status and comment) and also whether we wish to have our new comment and order status **Visible on Frontend** (meaning that our order status and comment are visible within the customers dashboard).

7. Once happy with our comment and notification settings we can click on **Submit Comment**, this will change our order status from processing to **Delayed** wherever our order status is displayed within the administration panel.

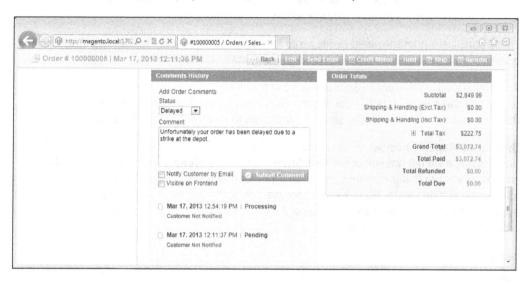

How it works...

Not all businesses can use the default Magento statuses to handle their orders, so it is important to know that we can break down each complex stage into separate statuses, keeping the customer informed of any problems that we as a business may encounter with their order.

To be able to effectively set up a new order status it is important to understand the difference between an **Order State** section and an **Order Status** section.

An **Order State** section is effectively the current core state that an order resides within—depending on what we have done with it. Within Magento these are broken down into eight different states:

- ▸ **New**: A new order comes into the system without any manual or automatic input

- ▸ **Pending payment**: An order has been created, but payment has not yet been captured (for example, check/money order)

- ▶ **Processing**: An order has started to be processed—normally, when either payment has been taken, the order has been invoiced or the order has been shipped

- ▶ **Complete**: Order has been invoiced and shipped

- ▶ **Closed**: Order has been closed after a successful credit memo

- ▶ **Cancelled**: Order has been canceled

- ▶ **On hold**: Order has been put on hold

- ▶ **Payment review**: Allows the order to be manually reviewed before payment taken—only if payment gateway allows this functionality

These states are primarily used by Magento and cover almost all the processing stages for our orders. Each of these states can hold as many statuses as we wish.

An order status is different to an order state in that a status is customer and administrator facing (we can see the label of the status). Statuses can be changed and created, whereas the core states must remain the same for Magento to process our orders correctly.

By default, Magento has set its own order status of processing to the order state processing and (because we did not select the **Use Order Status as Default** option when we created our new order status) this is currently the default status that will be applied when the order moves into the processing state. However because we now have our own custom order status also applied to the processing state, once an order moves into this state, we can now select either processing or delayed for its status.

There's more...

Each order state within Magento performs different actions on the way we interact with our orders—for example when an order is kept on hold, the customer cannot click on the **Reorder** button from within their dashboard, therefore when we are creating our custom order statuses, we must consider first the order state they are to be applied to.

Magento provides us with the ability to edit our **Order Status** labels for each store view on our Magento installation—this is helpful as we would not want to go to the trouble of creating a new customer facing order status if they could not read it in their chosen store language.

The following illustration shows a rough journey through the order states of Magento. The items with a star indicate an order state, the large dark line illustrates the ideal customer journey, whereas the other lines indicate the possible routes that an order can take, whether that be through canceling, putting the order on hold, or even refunding the order:

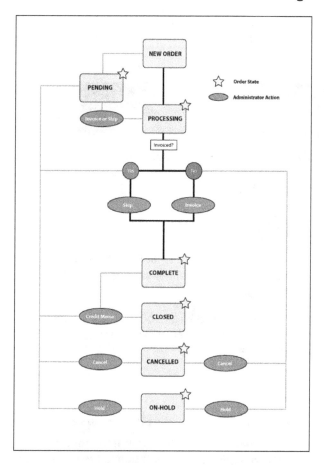

Reassigning our delayed status to the on hold state

If our order has been delayed realistically, the order should be within the on hold state. Previously, we had assigned our delayed status to our processing stage, but what happens if we choose to put that particular order on hold? Well, our custom status will be replaced with the default on hold status.

This is a good example of knowing which custom statuses should go with which stage.

To reassign the status to our on hold status we need to perform the following steps:

1. Navigate to **System | Order Statuses** and click on the **Unassign** link next to our **Delayed** status.

2. Click on **Assign Status to State**, set **Order Status** to **Delayed**, and **Order State** to **On Hold**.

Now when we hold our order (by clicking on the hold button on the order view page), we will be able to change our order **On Hold** status to **Delayed** by applying it within the comments history box as before.

Shipping promotions and discounts (Become an expert)

There are many tools available within Magento that can be used to increase conversion rates on the website. Shipping promotions and discounts are a fast, effective way of tempting customers to checkout through shipping offers.

Getting ready

For this exercise we will be using the Magento Flat Rate Shipping method. This technique will also work with any other shipping method, but to save us time in configuring our shipping rate spreadsheets we will use Flat Rate.

Our new free local shipping service will take into account the customer's address details when they order from our Magento store. For our example we are going to allow free shipping for anyone within the California area.

How to do it...

1. Navigate to **Promotions | Shopping Cart Price Rules** and click on **Add New Rule**.

2. Within the **Rule Information** tab inside **General Information** we need to set **Rule Name** to **Free Local Shipping** and **Description** to **Free local shipping for the good citizens of California!**.

3. Set **Status** to **Active** and **Websites** to **Main Website** (and any others we wish to apply it to), in **Customer Groups** select all customer groups, and finally, for **Coupon** select **No Coupon**.

4. Leave all other options within the **General Information** tab as default.

5. To specify the criteria that the customer needs to match before we grant them this promotion, we must first click on the **Conditions** tab and ensure the top line contains **If ALL of these conditions are TRUE** and then we click on the small green plus sign and select **Shipping State/Province**.

6. Next we must ensure that the following word after **Shipping State/Province** is **is** and then click on the **...** button (three small dots shown on screen) and select **California** from the list of states as shown in the following screenshot:

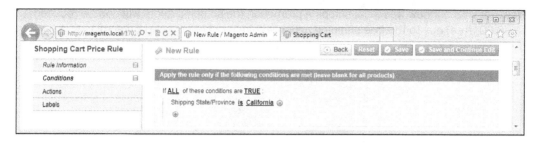

7. Now to specify the action that our coupon is going to undertake for our shopping cart, we must first click on the **Actions** tab and set **Free Shipping** to **For shipment** with matching items.

8. Each promotion can either act independently or alongside other promotions with their own rules, therefore to just provide our free shipping promotion for California to our customers we must set our **Stop further rules processing** to **Yes**, this will stop any other shopping cart price rule being applied if our current rule is triggered.

9. Finally, we need to enter our promotion label, so we must click on the **Labels** tab and set **Default Rule Label for All Store Views** to **Free Local Shipping**, and finally click on **Save**.

How it works...

On the shopping cart page, a customer can estimate their shipping and tax. Without our new promotion, the customer would receive the following quote and have to pay our standard Flat Rate fee of $5.00:

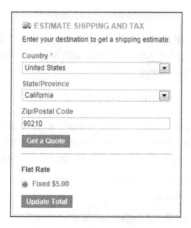

However with our new free local shipping promotion the shipping quote will now be reduced to $0.00 (free) due to the free shipping action within our shopping cart price rule as shown in the following screenshot:

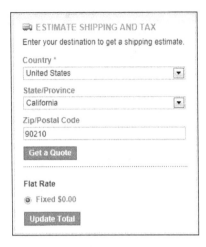

Shopping cart price rules offer a range of conditions, however our most important condition for this exercise was the ability to narrow down the conditions for the customer so that the **Shipping State/Province** section matched our criteria of **California**, and then within our **Actions** tab enabling free shipping by selecting **for shipment with matching items** (meaning any order because we had not specified any items that need to be matched—only the customers' state/province).

There's more...

There are lots of combinations of conditions that can be applied for creating discounts with your shipping costs and it is worth experimenting with a few of these conditions to create a promotion that is right for our business.

Shipping specific conditions include the following:

- ▶ **Subtotal**: Using the subtotal condition will allow us to perform promotion actions if the shopping basket is above a certain level. This is extremely useful if we wish to provide our free shipping action if the order value is greater than say $50.

- ▶ **Total items quantity**: Sometimes we may wish to provide a promotion if the customer purchases more than one item.

- ▶ **Total weight**: If our courier charges us by shipping weight then we may not wish to offer free shipping for anything above a certain weight threshold. This could be used in conjunction with another condition to act as a safe guard.

- ▸ **Shipping method**: Sometimes we may offer our customers multiple choices of couriers through separate shipping methods such as Table Rates or Flat Rate. If we wanted to, we could provide a promotion if a customer chooses a particular shipping method.

- ▸ **Shipping postcode**: Magento allows us to narrow down our criteria all the way to postcode. This would be useful if perhaps the customer lived in the same area as us, perhaps granting them free delivery for using their local business.

- ▸ **Shipping region**: Shipping region is used when a customer manually enters their state/province (that is, it does not allow a drop-down list, for example United Kingdom). Be careful if you rely on this however, as misspellings or typos by the customer will not trigger the promotion.

- ▸ **Shipping state/province**: As used in our example, this matches the customer's state/province from a drop-down list.

- ▸ **Shipping country**: We can specify different rules for different countries. This is useful if we are delivering internationally or even wish to restrict to our own country.

When editing our promotion actions, we can see that there is also an **Apply to Shipping Amount** option. This would take effect if we were providing a discount amount. The discount amount would be taken from the cart subtotal as well as the shipping charge.

Currently, there are a few disadvantages with the shopping cart price rules system, for our example we used shipping state/province to apply a free shipping charge—you will notice that not all of the world's states/provinces are listed—we are restricted by those that Magento provides for us. In order to add new states, countries, and regions to our list we need to edit the `directory_country_region` and `directory_country_region_name` database tables. Please ask your developer to insert into the database the values that you may require.

There is more information on shopping cart price rules (and the entire promotions system) at the following link:

`http://tinyurl.com/bporqqk`

Free shipping for all USA orders with more than five items

To extend our promotions we could look at offering free shipping to any USA order with five items or more in the cart. We will do this by creating another promotion, but this time within the **Conditions** tab we will enter the following:

1. The first line must say **If ALL of these conditions are TRUE**.

2. Then set **Shipping Country** to **United States** and **Total Items Quantity** to **equals or greater than 5**, finally click on **Save** as shown in the following screenshot:

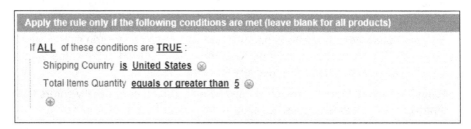

With those conditions and using the same data as we provided before, our new promotion will enable free shipping for all orders shipping to the USA with five or more items in the cart.

Free shipping for USA orders with no more than five items, total weight of greater than 10 kg, and an order value of less than $100

It is possible to create some rather complex promotions for our free shipping rule. For example if we were to only offer free shipping if the customer is spending a lot of money (over $100), the items that they have chosen are not heavy (total weight less than 10 kg) and that they have not chosen any more than five items, we could use the data shown in the following screenshot within the **Conditions** tab:

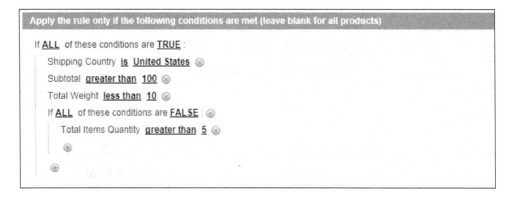

Notice that we can string together different condition branches. In our case we are testing that if the total items quantity is greater than five then we should fail our price rule—even if all the other criteria are matched.

Handling your shipping reports (Become an expert)

Reports are an important part of any business. Magento comes equipped with an entire reporting system that allows us to export our shipping reports.

Getting ready

To be able to generate the most recent data Magento will sometimes display a message (as shown in the following screenshot) advising us to refresh our statistics at the top of this page:

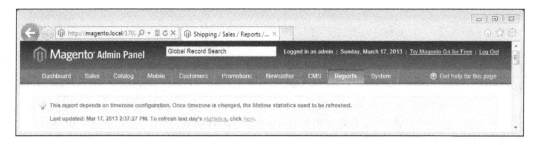

To refresh our statistics we can simply click on the links provided or navigate to **Reports | Refresh Statistics**.

Magento's shipping reports are there to give us a breakdown of all shipping methods/rates used within a certain period of time. This could be useful when figuring out for example, whether the Free Shipping method is more popular than the next day shipping method.

How to do it...

1. Navigate to **Reports | Sales | Shipping** and ensure that **Show Report For** is set to **All Websites** (if we wish to only show reports for a specific store we can do this here) and our **Match Period To** field should be set to **Order Created Date**.

2. Next set **Period** to **Day** and then select a date in the past by clicking on the calendar next to the **From** field, then select today's date from the **To** field and set **Order Status** to **Any** and **Empty Rows** to **No** as shown in the following screenshot:

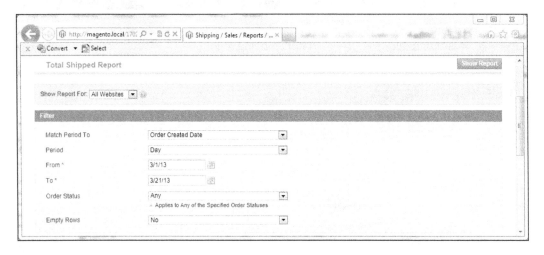

3. We can then click on **Show Report** to see our report and then to export the report we can choose **Export to CSV** and click on the **Export** button to download a CSV file of our data:

How it works...

The shipping reports that we can export from Magento only contain those orders, which have been shipped, or more specifically, all of our **Sales | Shipments**.

As we can see from the **Show Report** data, the report solely focuses on the shipping methods/rates used on any given shipment, combining them into days, and summing up the number of orders that used that particular method/rate.

There's more...

We can adjust our shipping reports to show particular order statuses—this is a great way of filtering out those shipments that have a particular custom status, for example our delayed custom status.

The Magento dashboard chart is a great tool that requires little configuration, but which can show us a cost breakdown for all of our shipments across a number of timespans. By navigating to our Magento dashboard we can see at a glance how much of our orders is made up of shipping charges. If we cannot see the chart, we may need to enable it by navigating to **System | Configuration | Admin | Dashboard** and selecting **Yes** for **Enable Charts**.

Customizing your shipping e-mails (Become an expert)

E-mailing a customer once their order has been shipped is a vital stage of any Magento website. The default new shipment template however, can sometimes be (to say the least) a little uninspiring. Within Magento lie the tools to edit our transactional e-mails to however we wish.

Getting ready

To be able to edit our transactional e-mails, a good working knowledge of HTML and CSS is required.

How to do it...

1. Navigate to **System | Transactional Emails** and click on **Add New Template**.
2. Under **Load default template,** select **New Shipment** from the **Template** drop-down menu and click on **Load Template**.
3. In the **Template Name** field enter `Custom New Shipment`.
4. Change the **Template Subject** field so that it reads as follows:

```
Your Order # {{var order.increment_id}} has been shipped!
(Shipment # {{var shipment.increment_id}})
```

5. Edit the HTML within the **Template Content** field so that the first line reads **Thank you for your order from {{var store.getFrontendName()}}, we can confirm that your order has now been shipped**. To save our new template click on **Save Template**:

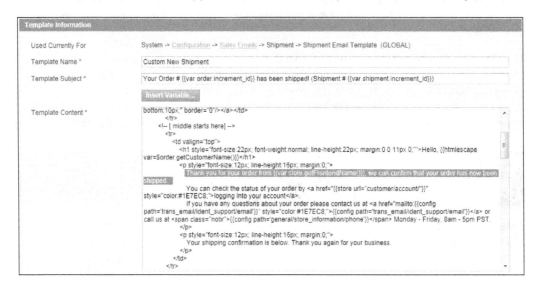

6. To assign our new template to our sales e-mail process we first need to navigate to **System | Configuration | Sales Emails** making sure that our scope is set to **Default Config** and then within the **Shipment** tab change the **Shipment Email Template** field to **Custom New Shipment**, finally click on **Save Config**:

How it works...

Once we have created our new shipment template and assigned it as our new shipment e-mail template, all new shipments that are created for our order will receive our new e-mail when the **Email Copy of Shipment** has been ticked when submitting the shipment:

Our changes will take effect immediately as we can see from this screenshot of the e-mail received:

Robs Clothing: New Order # 100000010

Robs Clothing: Invoice # 100000008 for Order # 100000010

Your Order # 100000010 has been shipped! (Shipment # 100000008)

There's more...

Transactional e-mails can be edited for all sorts of automatic e-mails, from invoices to credit memos. One thing to make sure of though is that we cater for guests as well as customers.

For each of the main transactional templates there is a guest and a non-guest version, so depending on our store setup (whether we allow guest to checkout) we need to ensure both templates have been edited.

There is more information on editing transactional e-mail templates at the following URL:

```
http://tinyurl.com/cvzwyzf
```

Using variables in transactional e-mails

An important thing to consider when editing the transactional templates is to ensure that all data remains consistent throughout the website. Magento provides variables for us to do this. Within our custom e-mail template there is a button called **Insert Variable...**, clicking this will bring up a list of variables that can be used inside the e-mail.

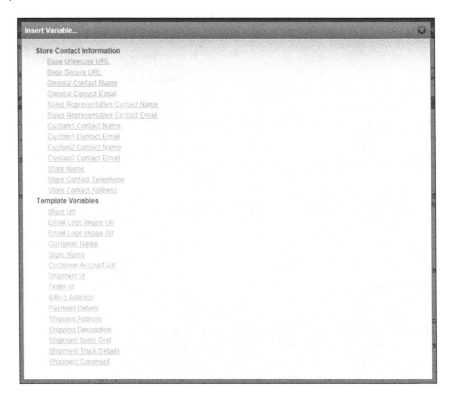

The value of each of these variables is contained within the store configuration, so as long as the variable is used on all templates we do not need to worry when changing, for example our **Store Contact Telephone** information.

 **Thank you for buying**
Instant Magento Shipping How-to

About Packt Publishing

Packt, pronounced 'packed', published its first book "*Mastering phpMyAdmin for Effective MySQL Management*" in April 2004 and subsequently continued to specialize in publishing highly focused books on specific technologies and solutions.

Our books and publications share the experiences of your fellow IT professionals in adapting and customizing today's systems, applications, and frameworks. Our solution based books give you the knowledge and power to customize the software and technologies you're using to get the job done. Packt books are more specific and less general than the IT books you have seen in the past. Our unique business model allows us to bring you more focused information, giving you more of what you need to know, and less of what you don't.

Packt is a modern, yet unique publishing company, which focuses on producing quality, cutting-edge books for communities of developers, administrators, and newbies alike. For more information, please visit our website: www.packtpub.com.

Writing for Packt

We welcome all inquiries from people who are interested in authoring. Book proposals should be sent to author@packtpub.com. If your book idea is still at an early stage and you would like to discuss it first before writing a formal book proposal, contact us; one of our commissioning editors will get in touch with you.

We're not just looking for published authors; if you have strong technical skills but no writing experience, our experienced editors can help you develop a writing career, or simply get some additional reward for your expertise.

Instant E-Commerce with Magento: Build a Shop

ISBN: 978-1-78216-486-9   Paperback: 52 pages

A fast-paced, practical guide to building your own shop with Magento

1. Learn something new in an Instant! A short, fast, focused guide delivering immediate results

2. Learn how to install and configure an online shop with Magento

3. Tackle difficult tasks like payment gateways, shipping options, and custom theming

Getting Started with nopCommerce

ISBN: 978-1-78216-644-3   Paperback: 116 pages

An in-depth, practical guide to getting your first e-commerce site up and running using nopCommerce

1. Learn to install and configure nopCommerce in order to start selling products online

2. Discover the key areas and features to get up and running fast

3. Learn how to create and manage products, shipping, and payment methods

Please check **www.PacktPub.com** for information on our titles

Mastering Magento

ISBN: 978-1-84951-694-5   Paperback: 300 pages

Maximize the power of Magento: for developers, designers, and store owners

1. Learn how to customize your Magento store for maximum performance

2. Exploit little known techniques for extending and tuning your Magento installation

3. Step-by-step guides for making your store run faster, better and more productively

Magento PHP Developer's Guide

ISBN: 978-1-78216-306-0   Paperback: 256 pages

Get started with the flexible and powerful e-commerce framework, magento

1. Build your first Magento extension, step by step

2. Extend core Magento functionality, such as the API

3. Learn how to test your Magento code

Please check **www.PacktPub.com** for information on our titles